And So to Bed

By Melanie Donovan
Illustrated by Oliver Orville

A GOLDEN BOOK · NEW YORK
Western Publishing Company, Inc., Racine, Wisconsin 53404

MCMXCIII

Evening has come. All the sleepy little animals are getting ready for bed. It is a peaceful time of stories and songs. I know stories about some animal friends of mine. Listen, and I will tell you.

The Bedtime Kitten

Suzi was a small kitten with a chocolate-colored nose and bright blue eyes. She loved to chase her yellow ball and eat from her own bowl. But most of all she liked to have Jessica scratch her just behind the ears.

"Whurr, whurr, whurr," Suzi purred as Jessica scratched behind the kitten's right ear.

"Oh, Suzi, you sound just like an electric fan," Jessica said.

At eight o'clock Jessica's mother called,
"Time to get ready for bed."

Jessica put on her pink pajamas,
brushed her teeth, and crawled into bed.
Suzi crawled into bed beside her.

Mother read a story and sang a song from Jessica's favorite book. Then she gave Jessica a big hug and a kiss and said, "Sleep tight! Don't let the bedbugs bite!

"Come on, Suzi, it's time for Jessie to go to sleep," whispered Mother. She scooped up the kitten and carried her downstairs.

Suzi didn't feel like playing with her yellow
ball, and she didn't feel like eating from her
own bowl. All she could think of was Jessica
scratching the spot behind her ear.

Up the stairs she padded. She pushed
Jessica's door open with her chocolate-
colored nose, and with one big jump she
landed on the bed.

"Oh, Suzi," said Jessica, yawning, as she slowly scratched just the right spot behind the kitten's right ear. "It must be your bedtime, too."

"Whurr, whurr, whurr!" purred Suzi.

And soon both Suzi and Jessica were sound asleep.

Sleepy Puppy

"And what has my little one been doing all this long day?" asked Mother Dog as Puppy settled himself for sleep. "Lots of things," said Puppy.

"I played chase-the-ball with the boy, and I brought the ball back every time, even when it rolled under the hedge.

"And I did not chase Suzi Kitten once
all day. I even let her play with my
squeaky mouse.

"I learned new words—

fetch,

stay,

and *get down.*

"I ate all my dinner and hardly spilled any. The boy's mother said I was a good dog.

"I was good, wasn't I, Mother?"

"Yes, my good sleepy puppy," said Mother Dog. "Now close your eyes and go to sleep."

And that is just what Puppy did. He closed his eyes and went to sleep. And so did his mother.

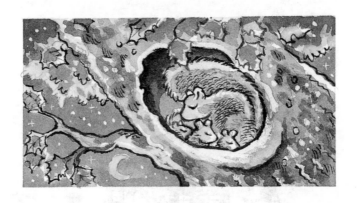

Sweet Dreams

All the wild animals safe at home dream of their favorite things.

The squirrel family in a hole in the old maple tree curl up under sweet-smelling leaves and dream of playing tag in the treetops.

The sparrow chicks high in their nest
tuck in their wings and dream of flying to
the stars.

The bunnies deep in a burrow beneath the hedgerow lie very still and dream of fields of clover in the sun.

In the woods the baby fawn nuzzles his mother's side and dreams of leaping over a clear cool stream.

Shhh. All the little
animals are just about asleep.
Their mothers sing them one
last song.

Cradle Song

Lullaby and good night,
With roses bedight,
With lilies bedecked
Is baby's wee bed.
Lay thee down now and rest,
May thy slumber be blest,
Lay thee down now and rest,
May thy slumber be blest.

…And so to bed.

Good night!

I See the Moon

I see the moon,
And the moon sees me.
God bless the moon,
And God bless me.

Anonymous

Good Night, Sleep Tight

Good night, sleep tight,
Don't let the bedbugs bite.
Do what's right with all your might
And wake up bright in the morning
    light.

Anonymous